What Would You Do?

Melanie Cannon

Balboa Press books may be ordered through booksellers or by contacting:

Balboa Press
A Division of Hay House
1663 Liberty Drive
Bloomington, IN 47403
www.balboapress.com
1 (877) 407-4847

ISBN: 978-1-9822-0960-5 (sc)
ISBN: 978-1-9822-0961-2 (e)

Print information available on the last page.

Balboa Press rev. date: 09/13/2018

BALBOA.
PRESS
A DIVISION OF HAY HOUSE

For my parents, Gary and Cheryl Cannon,
who taught me to love books.

What would you do if you just couldn't fail?

If in every adventure you
were sure to prevail?

If there were a rainbow down every trail,

With a big pot of gold or
a nice pint of ale?

Would you find a cure for cancer, take a rocket to the stars?

Climb a giant mountain, invent trash-fueled cars?

Tell someone you love them,
dare for a first kiss?

Quit your job and move to Maui
in a quest to find your bliss?

Would you eat nothing but pizza
for weeks and weeks on end?

Or get a tattoo of a cartoon
character right on your rear end?

Maybe learn to play the accordion
or do a perfect belly flop,

Open a gourmet candy store
or a vegan coffee shop.

Get a degree in astrophysics or
go to film school at NYU,

End a harmful relationship or open
your mouth and say what's true.

Now of course it isn't true that
we'll always succeed.

Learning to live with mistakes is
something all humans need.

But your answer to that question
holds a very important clue.

It's a hint to just what lies at
the very heart of you.

Maybe it's a problem you
simply must solve.

Perhaps something inside
you is ready to evolve.

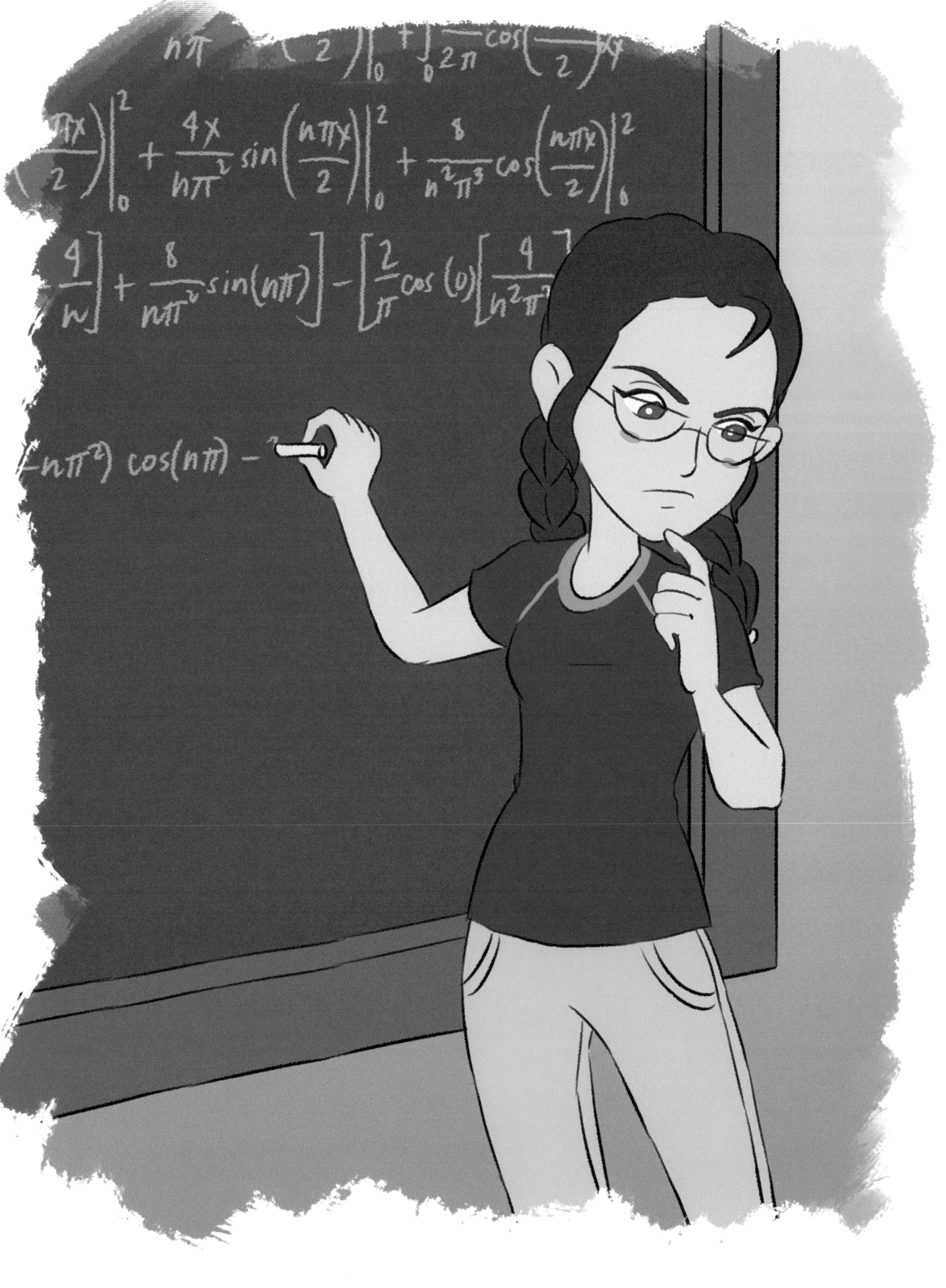

It could be time to fall in love or
to spend some time alone,

to set off on an adventure
or to cozy up at home.

It might be that you need
to exercise your mind,

Or listen to your heart and
leave logic far behind.

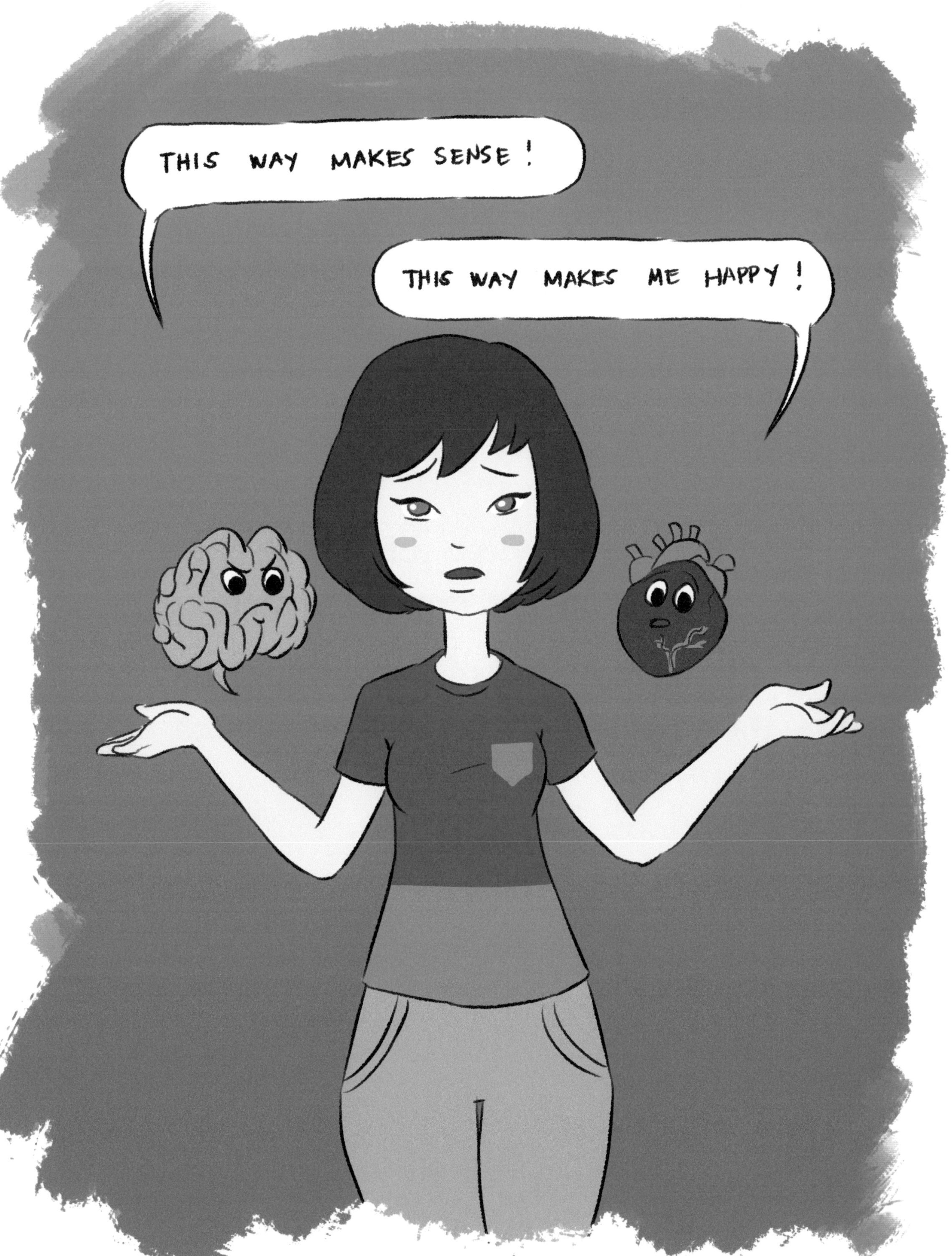
THIS WAY MAKES SENSE!
THIS WAY MAKES ME HAPPY!

You may just need a tweak or two
for your life and dreams to match,

Or you may have to throw the whole
thing out and start over from scratch.

And later you may find that
you need to rearrange.

Any day that you draw breath is
another chance to change.

You can create the life you
want and try it on for size,

then adapt it to accommodate
life's every surprise.

Maybe you aren't even
sure where to begin.

Guess what – you don't have to
know, you can just jump in!

Or just stick your toe in if
caution's more your style,

Make it a fun adventure,
not a dreadful trial.

It may sound oh-so-silly, but
I promise you it's not.

It's imperative that you truly live
this precious life you've got.

Because here's a truth about what we
need for this wonderful world to survive:

We need YOU, showing up,
ready, awake and alive!